Arise & Go
When a Nation in Need, Needs You

You're Invited Enterprises

Arise & Go
When a Nation in Need, Needs You

© 2024 by You're Invited Enterprises

ALL RIGHTS RESERVED

No part of this book may be reproduced or transmitted in any form or by any electronic or mechanical means, including storage or retrieval system, without permission in writing from the publisher, except in the case of brief quotations embodied in critical reviews or articles. For permission requests, write to the publisher, addressed "Permissions Request," at the below web address contact page.

You're Invited Enterprises
www.youreinvitedmag.com

Scripture quotations taken from the (NASB®) New American Standard Bible®, Copyright © 1960, 1971, 1977, 1995, 2020 by The Lockman Foundation. Used by permission. All rights reserved. www.lockman.org

THE HOLY BIBLE, NEW INTERNATIONAL VERSION®, NIV® Copyright © 1973, 1978, 1984, 2011 by Biblica, Inc.™ Used by permission. All rights reserved worldwide.

ISBN 979-8-218-44421-1

Table of Contents

1. CHAPTER ONE 08
   A Rebellious Heart on the Ship

2. CHAPTER TWO 22
   A Repented Heart in the Sea

3. CHAPTER THREE 36
   The Convicted Hearts in the City

4. CHAPTER FOUR 50
   The Compassionate Heart of God

   APPENDIX 62
   Inviting Jesus into Your Heart

   Tips for Hosting a Beach Themed Bible Study

Leaders

Pray

- Ask God to guide you as a leader in all aspects of this study.
- Pray for the women who will be attending.

Prepare

- Before beginning this study, review the material and activities. Be sure to prepare your ladies prior to that week's lesson, as needed.

Time

- Respect everyone's schedule by starting and ending on time.
- Keep the lesson moving and on topic. It's not necessary to discuss every question; however, it is beneficial to cover each day's material.

Sharing

- Create a safe atmosphere by letting the ladies know what is shared in the group stays in the group.
- It's okay if you don't have all the answers. Simply facilitate the discussion and let the Word of God speak for itself and be your guide.

Lastly, thank you for opening your heart and home (or church facility) for this bible study. May you and your ladies be blessed by it.

Introduction

Welcome to Arise and Go, a 4-week bible study on the book of Jonah. Perhaps you've heard this story before, and you think it's a bit fishy. After all, how many people are swallowed by a giant fish and live to tell the story? There is a great significance to that part of Jonah's ordeal, which you will discover, however, there is so much more to this tale than a man spending three days in the belly of a fish.

Over the next four weeks, we will cover one chapter at a time. Each chapter or lesson is broken into 5 days and will take approximately 30-40 minutes to complete. Some lessons include fun activities to support that week's message.

Our hope is that this bible study gives you a deeper understanding of God's Word. As Christians we sometimes skim through scriptures (or the internet) looking for a bible verse to hook us, when we could be diving deeper into God's Word. There's a big difference between snorkeling and scuba diving...DEPTH. Although both explore the seas observing spectacular marine life, scuba divers see so much more because of the depths in which they can travel. Similarly, when you dive deeper into God's Word you not only uncover a world of deeper wisdom and truth, you discover an amazing God!

So, let's spend time with Him and allow His truths to penetrate our hearts so our light can shine brighter in a world that is becoming increasingly darker, increasingly wicked!

Blessed is the nation whose God is the Lord.

Psalm 33:12

CHAPTER ONE

A Rebellious Heart on the Ship

Arise, go to Nineveh...but Jonah got up to flee to Tarshish from the presence of the Lord.
JONAH 1:2-3

Introduction

The book of Jonah may seem far-fetched to those who are critics of our faith. Jonah's oceanic event is indeed a larger-than-life story, but the bible – which is a compilation of writings - makes it clear that Jonah was a real person. The events that occurred in his life are true as written in the Word of God. But this book is so much more than a whale of a tale. Let's begin...

Day One

Whether or not you are familiar with this story, begin your time in prayer and ask the Lord to open your eyes and ears to what the Spirit of God is saying and what He wants you to learn this week.

Read Jonah 1, but please go no further. We want to unpack this book chapter by chapter. Then answer the questions below according to the text.

Jonah 1

1. What is Jonah told to do and by whom?

2. Why is Jonah told to go to the great city of Nineveh and cry out against it?

3. How does Jonah respond to his mission? Where is he headed?

4. What happened on his way to Tarshish?

5. How great was this storm and who caused it?

6. How do the sailors react to this calamity? Who do they turn to?

7. Where was Jonah during the storm? What was he doing?

8. How did they learn it was Jonah's fault for the storm? Note: we will learn more about this unfamiliar ancient practice on day 3, but for now, we just want you to list it below.

9. What does Jonah suggest they do to help calm the seas?

10. Why were the sailors afraid to follow through on Jonah's advice? What did they expect to happen to him?

11. What happened to the sea when Jonah was thrown overboard? Why were they extremely afraid?

12. According to verse 17 what happened to Jonah? How long?

13. After reading this chapter, what did you learn about God, Jonah and the sailors? List it on the next page.

<u>God</u>   <u>Jonah</u>   <u>Sailors</u>

We know a country's (or city's) wickedness can get out of control. We are seeing that every day on the news, but has it ever occurred to you that the Lord would step in to warn people of His impending judgment? Just as He did with Nineveh - the Word of God or the call to repentance, aptly spoken – has the power to convict a nation, causing them to turn from their evil ways. But first, God calls on His people, in Nineveh's case, Jonah – to arise and go.

Day Two

Was Jonah a real person or an imaginary one? Let's see what scripture says.

Reread Jonah 1 to refresh your memory.

The Prophet Jonah

1. In 2 Kings 14:23-25, we learn that during the reign of King Jeroboam II, Israel's borders were restored. According to verse 25, who prophesied this would occur?

2. Where was he from? Who was his father?

3. According to Jonah 1:1, was this the same prophet?

Cry Out Against the Great City

God calls on Jonah to cry out against the wicked city of Nineveh, the capital of Assyria, to rebuke their sin and repent. The Assyrians were enemies of Israel and were well known for their brutality. Every man was required to serve in the vast Assyrian army. They were well equipped with the latest military artillery and showed their adversaries no mercy. They often used psychological methods to torture their victims, such as skinning them alive, amputating their limbs, gouging their eyes, or impaling them on huge stakes, which ultimately caused a slow painful death. Many nations were terrified of the Assyrians! Jonah dispised them and didn't feel they were worthy of receiving God's mercy and grace.

1. The first mention of Nineveh is in the book of Genesis. After the flood, the sons of Noah and their children began to multiply and populate the land. Look up Genesis 10:8-11, and list what you learn about Nineveh?

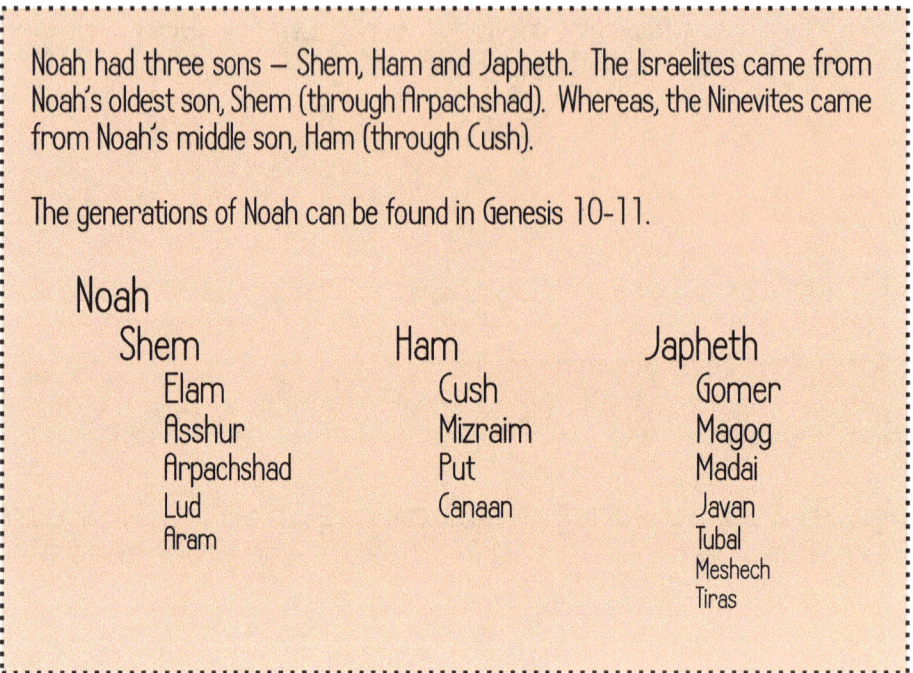

Although Jonah was commanded to cry out against Nineveh, other prophets of God have been called to speak against their own nation to get them to repent. What can we learn from them?

2. Look up the following scriptures and list what the prophets were told to do and/or proclaim:

- Isaiah 58:1

- Jeremiah 4:11-12, 14

- Matthew 3:1-2

- Ezekiel 33:10-11

Detour on the Mediterranean Sea

Instead of heading to Nineveh, Jonah flees to Tarshish from the presence of the Lord. Why Tarshish? First, as you can see on the map, it was in the opposite direction from Nineveh. Secondly, it was thought to be the farthest place before reaching the horizon and dropping off the ends of what was believed to be a flat earth. Although the exact location of Tarshish is unknown, many theologians believe it's probably in the area of Spain.

Jonah pays the fare and sets sail on a trip to Tarshish.

1. Read Ezekiel 27:25. How were the ships of Tarshish used to bring wealth to the city of Tyre? We will explore this more later in the week, so stay tuned.

Disobedience

Jonah wasn't just running from God's presence he was disobeying Him. The Lord called him to speak out against Nineveh because they needed to hear God's message, but instead Jonah took off in the opposite direction to the farthest place he could think of – Tarshish. However, Jonah is not the only one who has disobeyed the Lord.

1. According to Deuteronomy 28:15, what happens if the Israelites do not obey?

2. Look up Nehemiah 9:26-27. What happens when the people rebel?

3. Read 1 Samuel 15:1-3, 8-11, 20-23. How is rebellion viewed according to verse 23?

> The practice of divination is used to increase knowledge and understanding into future events through supernatural powers. Since divination is detestable to God (Deuteronomy 18:10-12), the insight or advice coming from these soothsayers is actually originating from demonic forces!
>
> Additional scriptures:
> - Leviticus 19:26, 31
> - Leviticus 20:6
> - Jeremiah 14:14

If the Lord called you to speak out against a wicked nation, how would you react? Would you follow through or would you – like Jonah – flee in the opposite direction?

Day Three

The Lord's presence is awesome and majestic. Why would anyone want to run away from His presence?

The Presence of the Lord

1. Read Genesis 3:8. What happened when Adam and Eve sinned? What was Jonah doing when he fled?

2. According to Genesis 4:8-16, what was Cain's punishment after he sinned?

3. Look up 2 Thessalonians 1:5-10. When Jesus returns what happens to those who don't know God nor obey the gospel (v. 9)?

4. According to Acts 3:19-20, what are we called to do so seasons of refreshment may come?

5. Read Psalm 97:1-6. The Lord Reigns! What happens in the presence of the Lord? How awesome must His presence be!

Over the Seas

Look up the following scriptures. What is the overall theme?

- Genesis 1:9-10, 21
- Psalm 135:6-7
- Psalm 95:5
- Psalm 146:5-6
- Psalm 65:5-8

1. Look up Nehemiah 9:6. Why was God able to stir up the sea and later calm it?

2. Read Psalm 107:23-31. According to verse 28, what did the people do? Who calmed the storm?

Prayer Meeting on Deck

The storm triggered fear in the sailors which caused them to cry out to their gods. However, Jonah (who knew the one true God) had fallen asleep below. The crew held a prayer meeting on deck, while Jonah was busy taking a nap. The one man who could do something did nothing because he was asleep. The unbelieving crew worked tirelessly to try and save Jonah's life, while he did little to try and save their souls by sharing the one true God with them.

What about you? Are you a sleepy Christian? Are you unaware of the chaos and confusion happening in the world because you're snoozing through it? Maybe it's time to get up on deck!

Casting Lots

1. Read Jonah 1:7. How do the sailors learn if was Jonah's fault?

When the sailors wanted to know who was responsible for the catastrophe, they cast lots, an unfamiliar term to us now, but was a common practice in ancient times. Certain objects — scholars believe may have been smooth stones with symbols on them or colored sticks — were used to determine an outcome from the gods (or God) on a particular subject matter or to answer a significant question.

Today the idea of casting lots may seem more like a game of chance or random luck than determining God's will. After all, we have the complete Word of God and the Holy Spirit to guide our decision making. However, in biblical times, the casting of lots was used when important decisions needed to be made. Although it may seem like a gamble, according to Proverbs 16:33, God controlled the outcome.

2. According to Acts 1:24-26, how was Matthias chosen as an apostle in place of Judas?

3. Look up Proverbs 16:33 and write it below.

Are you hiding? Do you have anything you need to confess before the Lord? Spend some time in prayer reflecting on all you've learned thus far.

Day Four
A Seaside Town

We have an informative activity for you today that will shed some light on Jonah 1.

Activity

Tyre was a seaside town, situated along the shoreline of the Mediterranean Sea, which allowed it to sell its merchandise to many nations and coastal towns. As a result of their rising trade, the nation became extremely prosperous and arrogant. Their pride became their downfall. God hates pride! Therefore, He gives His prophet Ezekiel a crushing message – Tyre will be utterly destroyed. Their ship (so to speak) is going to sink.

Since the ships of Tarshish were carriers of merchandise, we thought this activity would be helpful in light of Jonah. Read Ezekiel 27:1-25 and match the nation with the bartered goods. Answers at the end of the lesson (no peaking!).

	Nation		Bartered Goods
1.	Senir	A.	Ivory tusks & ebony
2.	Lebanon	B.	Horses & mules
3.	Bashan	C.	Silver, iron, tin & lead
4.	Cyprus	D.	Spices, precious stones & gold
5.	Egypt	E.	Saddle cloth/blankets
6.	Elishah	F.	Wine & white wool
7.	Tarshish	G.	Fir/pine trees
8.	Javan, Tubal & Meshech	H.	Fine embroidered linen
9.	Beth-Togarmah	I.	Turquoise, purple fabric, embroidered work, fine linen, coral & rubies
10.	Dedan/Rhodes	J.	Lambs, rams & goats
11.	Aram	K.	Cedar
12.	Judah	L.	Iron, cassia & sweet/aromatic cane
13.	Damascus	M.	Ivory/Cyprus wood
14.	Vedan & Javan (Danites & Greeks)	N.	Blue/purple clothing, embroidered garments & multicolored rugs/carpets
15.	Dedan	O.	Blue/purple fabric
16.	Arabia	P.	Oak
17.	Sheba & Raamah	Q.	Wheat, cakes, honey, oil & balm
18.	Haran, Canneh, Eden, Sheba, Asshur & Chilmad	R.	Slaves & bronze material

1. Based on what you learned about the merchandise the ships of Tarshish carried (along with the goods from Tyre), do you believe the cargo thrown overboard in Jonah 1:5 was just personal belongings or valuable merchandise? If the latter, how great would this loss be?

> In our world today, thousands of products are transported across the globe by cargo ships, airplanes, trains, and trucks. As a society we rely heavily on these shipping services to meet our day-to-day needs. When there are supply chain shortages or delays it can be challenging and problematic for many, just as it was in Jonah's day.

The Lord caused a great tempest on the sea. The storm was so catastrophic that the sailors began throwing the cargo overboard to save the ship. This turned out to be extremely costly for everyone. First, Jonah's disobedience brought harm to innocent sailors, whose lives were at risk. Secondly, precious cargo was tossed into the ocean to lighten the load, which might not have been needed had Jonah obeyed the Lord.

Day Five

God spoke through stormy weather to get Jonah's attention and bring about his repentance. Often times it's during the storms of life we hear God the loudest. It's during calamity, when our ship may be on the brink of breaking apart, that draws us to our knees and closer to God.

Discipline

1. Look up Proverbs 3:12 and Hebrews 12:5-8. To whom does the Lord discipline and why?

2. From what you've learned, how did God discipline Jonah?

3. How do you respond when the storms of life hit?

A Private Underwater Guesthouse

We want you to see something that you may or may not have picked up on. Reread Jonah 1:10-17 and fill in the blanks below.

¹² And he said to them, "_____ and _____.

Then _____ will become _____,

because I know that on account of me this great storm has come upon you."

¹⁵ So they _____ and _____,

and the _____ its raging.

Jonah didn't jump overboard. He had to be "picked up" and thrown into the ocean, which terrified the sailors. They were fearful they would be held responsible for Jonah's death. Out of options and desperate for relief, the sailors eventually toss Jonah into the raging ocean.

Now the Lord had a rather unusual deep-sea adventure in store for Jonah. One that entailed a three-night stay at a secluded underwater guesthouse. The Lord booked the private accommodations and made sure Jonah checked in. Though his stay was completely free, it would cost Jonah nearly everything. It was a lesson he'd never forget.

Although scripture says this was a great fish, the Hebrew definition does allow for any *fin moving creature*. Therefore, it's certainly possible Jonah may have been swallowed by a whale, as some have suggested. The biggest whale, and largest animal ever created, is the blue whale. Its length ranges somewhere between 80-100 feet, which is roughly the size of three school buses! The blue whale is also known as a Baleen whale because it has baleen plates rather than teeth. As the whale swallows (not chews) tiny crustaceans, these comb-like plates filter out the seawater from the food. Even more interesting, these creatures have more than one stomach. Whether it was a whale or a very large fish that God intentionally selected for this occasion, one thing is clear – God is going to use this event in an amazing way, so stay tuned.

Closing

We've covered a lot of ground this week, but so has Jonah. One day he's lying in bed and the next he's in the belly of a giant fish. Trapped. Troubled. Terrified. And in deep water! Not exactly the Mediterranean cruise he envisioned. Then again, the great city of Nineveh was drowning in wickedness and was in deep trouble too. God cared deeply about the Ninevites and told His servant Jonah to warn them and call them to repent. Instead, Jonah disobeyed God and it almost cost him his life. Now Jonah must obey God, but first deal with his sin and the consequences.

Answers:
1G, 2K, 3P, 4M, 5H, 6O, 7C, 8R, 9B, 10A, 11I, 12Q, 13F, 14L, 15E, 16J, 17D, 18N

He caused the storm to be still, so that the waves of the sea were hushed.

Psalm 107:29

CHAPTER TWO
A Repented Heart in the Sea

I remembered the LORD, and my prayer came to You, into Your holy temple.
JONAH 2:7

Introduction

Have you ever felt stuck? Trapped? Caught in a situation – whether or not it was of your own making – and you didn't know what to do, where to go, or how you were going to get through it? You are not alone. Jonah had gotten himself into a real jam! Stuck in the belly of a giant fish with nowhere to go. So he did the only thing he could, he cried out to God.

Day One

Read Jonah 1 to refresh your memory. Then read chapter two but go no further. Answer the questions below.

Jonah 2

1. When does Jonah begin to pray and why?

2. How is he feeling?

3. How dire was his situation before he was swallowed by the big fish?

4. How far had he sunk?

5. According to verse 9, what is Jonah attitude?

6. How did Jonah make it out alive?

7. Did God answer Jonah's prayer?

8. From whom does salvation come from?

9. What caused the fish to vomit up Jonah? What does that say about His power?

10. Although Jonah had disobeyed God and was swallowed by a great fish, where was God in all this?

Thrown into the raging sea, Jonah must have thought he was going to die. Instead of drowning, he now finds himself in an awkward situation - trapped in the belly of a fish. Entombed. But he knows the God of heaven who made the sea and every living creature, and he prays to the One who can save him.

Are you battling the raging seas of life, struggling to stay above water? Feeling like you are about to be swallowed up by your circumstances? Cry out to God, for only He can truly calm the seas of your life!

When you pass through deep waters, I will be with you.

Isaiah 43:2

Day Two

Today, we're going to look a little closer at the prayer Jonah prayed after he was tossed into the ocean. Fading away and barely alive, he finds himself alone and trapped in the belly of a fish. Out of distress, he cries out to God.

Reread Jonah 2. Now rewrite each verse in your own words. Try and grasp the gravity of what Jonah is going through as he sinks down into the depths of the vast ocean.

v. 1 _____

v. 2 _____

v. 3 _____

v. 4 _____

v. 5 _____

v. 6 _____

v. 7 _____

v. 8 _____

v. 9 _____

v. 10 _____

1. What stood out the most to you?

2. Were you able to comprehend what Jonah was going through? Explain how you think he felt and the struggle he went through as he tried to hang on to his life.

3. Did writing help you grasp Jonah's situation more clearly?

Prayer

1. Read Psalm 145:18-19. Does God hear our cries for help?

2. Look up the following scriptures and list why God wouldn't hear one's prayers?
   - Isaiah 59:1-2
   - Micah 3:4
   - Psalm 66:18

3. According to 1 John 1:9, what can one do about it?

Prayer gives us a unique opportunity to connect with the Creator of the Universe. To speak with the One who created the sea and affixed its boundaries, knowing He will answer our prayers according to His perfect will. Oh, what a powerful weapon we have in our toolbox. If only, we'd use it more often.

Day Three

Have you ever thought about what it must have been like for Jonah once he was trapped in the fish? Troubled. Worried. Scared and all alone. Stuck in an abode where endless darkness filled the confined space. Entombed and miserable. His surroundings were uncomfortable, gross, and definitely wet! Those were the longest three days of Jonah's life.

Save Me

1. According to Psalm 46:1-3, who is our refuge in times of trouble?

2. Read Exodus 15:1-2. What did God do to Pharaoh's army? What was the Israelites response?

3. Look up the below scriptures. How is the Psalmist's cry like Jonah's?

   - Psalm 69:1-2
   - Psalm 116:3-4
   - Psalm 30:2-3
   - Psalm 31:21-22
   - Psalm 86:13

The Depths of Sheol

The Hebrew word *Sheol* is found only in the Old Testament and denotes the place where the dead reside, whether good or bad. Old Testament believers trusted God would not abandon them to Sheol (Psalm 16:10-11), but raise their souls to life. In the New Testament, the Greek word used is *Hades* and it carries a similar meaning – the place of departed souls, whether good or bad. These two words are essentially the same - one deriving from the Greek language, while the other from Hebrew. Both refer to the life hereafter. In English, these words may be translated as grave or pit, but should not be confused with hell (*gehenna* in Greek). Hell is the final resting place where the ungodly dead will face their eternal punishment!

Look up the below scriptures and record what you learn about Sheol.

- 1 Samuel 2:6
- Psalm 6:4-5
- Psalm 86:12-13

As Jonah descended to the depth of Sheol, he says "the earth with its bars was around me forever. (Jonah 2:6)" What might these bars be?

1. Look up Matthew 16:18 and fill in the blank below.

    ...and the _____ of _____ will not overpower it.

2. Read Revelation 1:17-18. What does the living One (Jesus) have over death and Hades?

Jonah expected to die when he was thrown overboard and the waves pulled him under. The ocean – a place of death for Jonah – was comparable to Sheol. Had it not been for God's intervention, he would have drowned. However, God saved him by designating a giant sea creature (one He created) to swallow Jonah. Now God is going to use this encounter, not only as a way to discipline Jonah but as a sign. One you'll learn more about tomorrow.

Day Four & Five

During Jesus' ministry, He performed many miraculous signs and wonders that left the crowds amazed! He turned water into wine. He healed the sick. And He walked on water, just to name a few. On one particular occasion when the scribes and Pharisees were questioning Jesus' divine authority, they asked for a sign. The sign Jesus provides is quite meaningful and involves Jonah. Let's continue and learn how those scribes and Pharisees got schooled!

Sign of Jonah

Look up the below scriptures and answer the questions below.

- Matthew 12:38-40
- Matthew 16:4
- Luke 11:29-30

1. How does Jesus refer to those asking for a sign? Remember, He knows their hearts.

2. What sign is given?

3. How does the sign of Jonah compare to the Son of Man (Jesus)?

In the below chart, look up the scriptures and provide your answers.

Question	Jonah	Jesus
HOW: Jonah nearly die / Jesus died	Jonah 1:15; 2:2-3	Acts 2:22-23
WHERE: Entombed	Jonah 1:17	Luke 23:50-53
TIME: How long?	Jonah 1:17	Matthew 27:64; 28:1-8
HOW: Brought to life	Jonah 2:10	1 Corinthians 15:3-4

Jonah didn't physically die, Jesus did. Jonah <u>nearly</u> died in the ocean because of his sin; laid in the belly of an extraordinary fish, and was brought forth to life when the fish three days later vomited him onto the sand. In contrast, Jesus died for all our sins on the cross, laid in an empty tomb and three days later rose from the dead! Hallelujah! Jesus was the long-awaited Messiah. He was the heavenly sign they were looking for! Sadly, the religious leaders missed it.

1. How do these verses authenticate Jonah's story and confirm he truly was a real person?

Three Days and Three Nights

The bible makes it clear that Jonah was in the belly of the fish three days and three nights. Jesus confirms this when asked for a sign. "...but none will be given it except the sign of the prophet Jonah. For as Jonah was three days and three nights in the belly of a huge fish, so the Son of Man will be three days and three nights in the heart of the earth," (Matthew 12:39-40). If Jesus died on Friday and rose from the grave on Sunday, many make the three-day connection, but have difficulty coming to terms with three nights. Yet Jesus said it. He clearly compared His burial and resurrection to Jonah's encounter. So how do we rectify this timeline?

The most reasonable and logical explanation comes from F. LaGard Smith's commentary from The Daily Bible (Harvest House Publishers). If you're not familiar with The Daily Bible, we highly recommend it. It is arranged chronologically and comprised of 365 readings, so you read the entire bible in a year. Commentary by Mr. Smith is provided to help bridge any gaps or prepare the reader for what they're about to read. It is through his commentary on Jesus' final week that helps provide clarity into the three-night dilemma.

Here is our summary along with some additional information.

First, it's important to note how Jews determine time. In fact, it's essential. In Genesis 1, the first six days are summarized with the saying, "and there was evening and morning the <u>first</u>* day." Therefore, the Jewish day begins the day before at sunset (after the first three medium stars appear in the sky) and goes until the following day. Twilight is considered the time between the sun setting and the appearing of the third star.

Secondly, Passover is celebrated on the 14th day of Nissan (formally known as Abib). According to Exodus 12:1-15, each Jewish household was to take a male lamb without defect on the 10th day and care for it until the 14th day of the month. During this time, the lamb would be examined to make sure it was without defect. Then on the 14th day, the lamb would be slaughtered at twilight. Later that night – which according to Jewish time would technically be the 15th day – they would eat the

Passover meal. Every year, the Passover was to be celebrated throughout the generations as a lasting ordinance. It's a reminder of when God delivered the Israelites from Egyptian captivity.

When Jesus entered Jerusalem, the Sunday before He died, the crowds praised Jesus as King and worshipped Him with palm branches. It is commonly referred to as Palm Sunday. If this day is to be regarded as the 10th day when the lambs were selected – or in Jesus' case, the Lamb of God considered – then the 14th day would be Thursday. With this in mind, the explanation of three days and three nights becomes clear. Per the Jewish calendar, the day begins at sunset the night before, therefore, Thursday night would actually be considered the start of Friday as seen in the colored chart below.

*The sequence of the day (first, second, third, etc.), according to Genesis 1.

Wednesday	Thursday	Friday	Saturday	Sunday
Morning 13	Morning 14	Morning 15	Morning 16	Morning 17
Twilight	Twilight (Jesus dies)	Twilight	Twilight	Twilight
Evening/Begins Thursday 14	Evening/Begins Friday 15 — Jesus is buried, Passover Meal	Evening/Begins Saturday 16	Evening/Begins Sunday 17	Evening/Begins Monday 18

Day 1   Day 2   Day 3

Closing

Jonah nearly died when he was tossed into the ocean because of his sin. Had it not been for God's intervention, he would have drowned. Now entombed in the belly of a fish, in the heart of the sea for three days and three nights, he cries out to God. He prays to the only One who is truly able to save and restore his life. And God renews it. Even more astonishing is Jonah's ordeal remains forever linked to the Messiah's burial and resurrection! How awesome is that!

Christ died for our sins, and He was buried, and He was raised on the third day according to the scriptures.

1 Corinthians 15:3-4

CHAPTER THREE
The Convicted Hearts in the City

When God saw their deeds, that they turned from their evil way, then God relented of the disaster which
He had declared He would bring on them. So He did not do it.
JONAH 3:10

Introduction

Trouble is mounting. Intensifying. The abhorrent wickedness of Nineveh has provoked the Lord's anger. The city and its inhabitants are on the verge of annihilation and the people are unaware of it. They carry on with their reckless behavior, not knowing what lies ahead. If nothing changes, destruction is imminent. God is just. He cannot – and will not – allow their evil deeds to continue. However, God is also compassionate and merciful, so He informs His newly restored prophet to arise and go. He's got an important message for Jonah to deliver.

Day One

As we mentioned at the beginning of this study, we want to uncover this book chapter by chapter. Read Jonah 3 and answer the questions below.

Jonah 3

1. What is Jonah's response when the word came to him a second time?

2. What does God tell him to do?

3. What do you learn about Nineveh?

4. What was God's message to Nineveh?

5. Who responded first to the message? What did they do?

6. How does the king respond? What action does he take?

7. Did the people take the message seriously? Did they heed the warning?

8. According to verse 7-8, what four things are the people told to do? List them below.

9. How long had God given them to turn from evil? If not, what would happen?

10. What caused God to change His mind and not destroy the Ninevites?

With the message delivered, Nineveh is on its way to redemption. Tomorrow will look at other times when God had a message for His people, who were not listening.

Day Two

Today we are going to look at some cross-references. Before we get started, reread Jonah 3 to familiarize yourself with the chapter.

Listen Up

1. Look up Jeremiah 26:2-3. What does God tell His prophets to do? Why?

2. God sent His prophet, Ezekiel, to speak to the Israelites. According to Ezekiel 2:7, what was he told to do even if the people didn't listen?

3. Read Jeremiah 40:2-3. What happens when the people do not listen?

Calamity is Coming

1. According to Amos 3:6-7, if a disaster occurs in a city, who causes it to occur? Does the Lord send anyone to warn them?

2. Look up the verses below and list what you learn. Think about the cause and effect.

    a) Jeremiah 18:7-8

    b) Jeremiah 18:9-10

    c) Jeremiah 18:11

3. Read Exodus 32:1-14.

    a) What had the Israelites done to make God angry?

    b) What was He ready to do?

    c) Why did He change His mind?

    d) Do people today have idols – whether tangible or not – that may cause the Lord's anger to burn against them (individually or collectively)?

4. According to Jeremiah 16:10-13, what was the reason the Israelites were experiencing calamity? What had their forefathers done? What had they done?

5. Look up Joel 2:12-14. What does the Lord desire most when a person or nation strays from Him?

6. Read Isaiah 45:5-7. What do you learn about God?

7. Based on all you've learned, why does God allow calamity to occur? Does He warn the people beforehand? What do you think His purpose is in allowing these things to happen?

Do you view life and the world in general through the lens of scripture? Do you understand that sometimes (not always) God uses or allows calamity – sword (war), famine (food shortage), and plague (disease) – as a means of bringing judgement against a sinful nation? As you ponder these thoughts, use the space below to write anything that might be tugging on your heart.

Day Three

The King of Nineveh issued a strong edict. If the people didn't take it seriously, they would all lose their lives and there would be no country to rule. It was a desperate call to action and the Ninevites didn't know if God would relent or not. It was a wait and see moment...and their lives hung in the balance.

Sackcloth & Fasting

1. Read Esther 3:1 - 4:3. Through a deceptive act, the king issues an irrevocable decree to allow the annihilation of the Jewish people living in the land and the seizure of their property. How do the Jews, including Mordecai, respond? Note: This is a good example of what takes place when one puts on sackcloth and fasts, so take note.

2. Look up Daniel 9:3-6, 9-19.

   a) After Daniel realizes the Israelites would be in captivity for 70 years, he seeks the Lord through prayer. How does putting on sackcloth, sitting in ashes and fasting fit in?

   b) What does he say in his prayers to the Lord?

Spend Time in Prayer

Yesterday, you saw how God used calamity to bring judgement against a nation. List some things going on in the world today, that may provoke the Lord's anger.

Do you feel your country is headed in the wrong direction? Do you feel the Lord's wrath has been aroused due to its sinful behavior? Spend the rest of your time today praying on behalf of your country, its leaders, and fellow citizens. Use the space below to journal your prayer to the Lord.

Day Four & Five

Over the next two days, we are going to look at five kings who, at one point in their life, made a wise decision. Begin your time in prayer and ask the Lord to open your heart to what he wants you to learn through this study.

Five Kings

King Ahab

Ahab was the most wicked king to rule the Northern Kingdom, Israel. He was responsible for introducing the Israelites to Baal worship, causing them to sin. He did more than all the other kings before him to provoked the Lord's anger. One day, King Ahab took possession of another man's vineyard he had been coveting. As a result of his actions God sent the prophet, Elijah, to confront him.

Read 1 Kings 21:1-29.

1. Why was the Lord angry with King Ahab? How had he obtained this vineyard?

2. What does the Lord plan to do to punish him?

3. What does Ahab do that caused the Lord to change His mind?

4. According to verse 29, is justice still carried out by a just God? Remember, the Lord knows a man's heart (even Ahab's son who will succeed him one day).

King Hezekiah

Hezekiah became king when he was 25 years old. He did what was right in the sight of the Lord and tore down the high places where the Israelites worshipped their foreign gods. He trusted in the Lord and kept His commands.

There came a day when King Hezekiah fell ill and was close to death's door. The prophet, Isaiah, told him to put his house in order for he would die. Heartbroken,

Hezekiah wept. The Lord heard his prayer and added 15 more years to his life. Yet, despite all the Lord did for him, later on the king became prideful.

Read 2 Chronicles 32:25-26.

1. Why did the Lord's wrath come upon him?

2. What did he do that changed things?

King Nebuchadnezzar

Nebuchadnezzar was a great and mighty king who ruled over Babylon. One night, the king had a dream that disturbed him terribly. Unable to understand it, he called all the wise men together to see if any of them could interpret the dream. Daniel, a man of God, was able to understand and interpret the dream for the king.

Read Daniel 4:19-27.

1. What was going to happen to the king?

2. In verse 27, what advice does Daniel give the king?

Read Daniel 4:28-37.

3. What was on the king's mind as he walked on the rooftop of the palace?

4. According to Daniel 4:25, what did the king need to recognize?

5. What happened to him (verses 31-32)?

Have this attitude in yourselves which was also in Christ Jesus, who, although He existed in the form of God, did not regard equality with God a thing to be grasped, but emptied Himself, taking the form of a bond-servant and being made in the likeness of men. And being found in appearance as a man, He humbled Himself by becoming obedient to the point of death, even death on a cross.

Philippians 2:5-8

6. According to verse 34, what changed in Nebuchadnezzar?

7. Who does King Nebuchadnezzar exalt and why?

Look up Daniel 4:37 and fill in the blanks below.

"Now I Nebuchadnezzar praise, exalt, and honor the _____ for all His works are _____ and His ways _____, and He is able to _____ those who _____."

King Josiah

At the age of eight, Josiah was just a child when he became king. He did right in the eyes of God and turned to Him with all his heart, all his soul, and all his strength. During his reign, he set out to purify the land and commissioned men to repair the temple. While there, the men found the book of the Law in the Lord's house which had been neglected.

Read 2 Chronicles 34:16-21, 26-28.

1. What does the king do when he hears the words of the Law?

2. What is going to happen to the people because they have forsaken the Lord and worshipped other gods?

3. According to verse 27, how had the king's actions delayed the Lord's wrath?

King of Nineveh

Headed for annihilation, the King of Nineveh was given just 40 days to heed the warnings. Quick decisive righteous action was critical at this time, otherwise, the wrath of God would be poured out on the city. The king had to get it right. And there were no guarantees!

Reread Jonah 3. Pay close attention to the king's actions.

1. How does the king respond to the news?

2. Do you see any resemblance to what the other four kings did? List the similarities.

3. Had the King of Nineveh shown humility?

Based on all you've learned, what had these five leaders done that changed their circumstances? Do you really think something so simple could change the direction of a sinful nation?

Judgment Day

Last week you looked at the sign of Jonah and how Jesus compared it to His burial and resurrection. Read the scriptures below and answer the questions.

- Matthew 12:38-41
- Luke 11:29-32

1. According to Matthew 12:41 and Luke 11:32, what will the men of Nineveh do on the day of judgment?

2. Why do you suppose that happens?

Closing

The wicked city of Nineveh was in serious trouble. Their evil deeds were rampant and had provoked the Lord's anger. If they did not repent, He would obliterate them. Truly God did not want any of them to perish (2 Peter 3:9), rather He wanted them to turn from their wicked ways. Therefore, He sent His servant Jonah to warn them.

Surprisingly, the people believed the alarming message and took action. They fasted, put on sackcloth, and humbled themselves. They even called on their fellow citizens – from the greatest to the least – to do the same. Even the king was convicted and issued a strong proclamation. As a result, the Ninevites turned away from their sinful ways and fervently called on God. But as the clock ticked down, the people had no idea if God would relent. All they could do is wait and see.

> When God saw their deeds, that they turned from their evil way, then God relented of the disaster which He had declared He would bring on them. So, He did not do it.
>
> Jonah 3:10

CHAPTER FOUR

The Compassionate Heart of God

...You are a gracious and compassionate God, slow to anger and abundant in mercy and One who relents of disaster.
JONAH 4:2

Fun Activity on Day 4

Introduction

When Jonah brought forth God's message to Nineveh, he had no idea if the people would repent. But if they did, he knew God would forgive them. He knew the Lord was a gracious and compassionate God. After all, God spared his life when he was in the belly of a fish due to his own rebellion. However, if the Ninevites continued in their wicked ways, Jonah knew God would bring about their destruction in 40 days and he would be absolutely delighted because he despised them. After all, they were Israel's greatest adversary. They were known for being ruthless and brutal in their treatment of their enemies. Much to his dismay, the people repented and Jonah, instead of rejoicing, was furious.

Day One

Read Jonah 4 and answer the questions below.

1. Why was Jonah angry?

2. List what you learn about God.

3. What was the real reason Jonah fled to Tarshish?

4. Why do you suppose Jonah wanted to die?

5. When Jonah left the city (v.5), what was he hoping would happen to the people?

6. Why was Jonah overjoyed with the plant?

7. What happened to the plant and who caused it? By what means?

8. What happened when the sun came up?

9. Did Jonah have reason to be angry? What does Jonah's attitude reveal about his focus?

10. Do you think this was pleasing to God?

11. What should our attitude be toward the unsaved?

Day Two

Anger

1. Look up Ephesians 4:25-27, 31-32. Is it okay to be angry? What guidance is provided?

2. Based on Psalm 30:4-5, what do you learn about God's anger?

3. According to Colossians 3:8, what are believers instructed to put aside? List them below.

4. Galatians 5:19-24. In which category does outburst of anger fall?

5. Read James 1:19-20. How should one handle their anger? What does man's anger not achieve?

6. How would you compare Jonah's anger to God's anger?

What about you? Is there anything building up within your heart that needs to be addressed? Do you ever get mad or have outbursts of anger? It's okay to be angry, God understands. But you cannot let it fester and become sin. Confess it before the Lord and ask Him to fill your heart with love and compassion.

Jonah's Compassion

Jonah gives God's edict to the people of Nineveh. They have 40 days to turn from their wicked ways or be destroyed. Jonah leaves the city and finds a place nearby to see what would happen (v. 5). To his surprise, the Ninevites respond appropriately to the message. Thus, Jonah is annoyed the people may actually be spared from judgment. He is angry with God for being so compassionate towards them. In fact, Jonah is so miserable he would rather die than live. Whereas the Ninevites are so alarmed they would rather live than die.

Reread Jonah 4:5-11 and answer the following questions.

1. What happens while Jonah waits to see what transpires to Nineveh?

2. What does Jonah have compassion for?

3. Who does God have compassion for?

4. How would you compare Jonah's focus to God's focus?

Jonah had more compassion for a plant that grew overnight and perished the following day than he did for the lost souls of Nineveh. He didn't feel they deserved to be shown mercy. Yet God had sympathy for them. Just as He had compassion for us, for while we were still sinners, Christ died for us.

Day Three

God cares about all people – Jew and Gentile, Israelite and Ninevite. One of the reasons Jonah fled to Tarshish was because he knew God's character. He knew the Lord would have compassion on the Ninevites if they turned from their wicked ways. And even if they didn't turn away from evil, God still showed compassion by sending His servant, Jonah, to warn them.

God's Compassion

1. Look up Psalm 103:8 and write it below.

2. Read Psalm 51:1. According to what two things does God blot out our transgressions?

3. Read Genesis 19:12-22. How did God's messengers display compassion towards Lot and his family? How swift was this judgement coming?

4. Look up Nehemiah 9:16-27. How did God demonstrate His love and compassion towards the Israelites? List them below.

5. According to 2 Chronicles 36:14-16, why does the Lord continue to send messengers to warn the people? How does this reflect His character?

6. In Psalm 103:13, what does God's compassion compare to? Who does the Lord have compassion for?

7. Read Psalm 86:1-10. According to verse 5, what do you learn about God?

Compassion for the Lost

According to Jonah 4:11, there were more than 120,000 souls who didn't perish because of God's compassion and mercy.

Reread Jonah 4:11, noting what they do not know. Then look up the following scriptures:

- Deuteronomy 1:39
- Isaiah 7:16

1. Based on what you've learned, how old do you suppose the 120,000+ souls were?

    o Babies/Young Children
    o Teens/Teenagers
    o Young Adults/Adults
    o Seniors/Elderly

These and others would have perished if Jonah had not shared God's Word to the lost. The same holds true for you, too. Are you withholding God's Word from the unsaved?

For I am not ashamed of the gospel, for it is the power of God for salvation to everyone who believes, to the Jew first and also to the Greek.

Romans 1:16

Day Four

Like Jonah, you can make a difference. You can make an impact on someone's life. The Story of the Sea Star (also called the Starfish Story) is a simple tale that reinforces this truth. The story has been told in various forms and is an adaptation from The Star Thrower by Loren Eisley.

The Story of the Sea Stars

It was a beautiful day when we decided to take our two grandkids to the beach to play in the sand and enjoy the afternoon sun. We grabbed our beach towels, sunscreen, their plastic pails with shovels and headed down to the beach. When we arrived, we noticed numerous starfish along the shoreline.

"What are they, Pops?" my grandson asked.

"They're sea stars, but most people call them starfish," he replied.

My granddaughter asked why they were on the beach instead of in the water where they belonged. He told her they must have washed ashore during the recent storm.

"What's going to happen to them?" they both asked.

"Well, if they don't make it back to the water, they won't survive the hot sun," he replied, "the sea is their home."

"You mean they're going to die?" they said with great sadness. "We've got to help them get back to their home!"

"What can we do, Grandma?" my granddaughter turned to me and asked. At this point I wasn't sure we could do anything. There were so many starfish that it would be impossible to save them all. Besides, I didn't want the kids touching them, so I told them there wasn't much we could do and encouraged them to play in the sand. We laid our towels down and settled in. Pops watched the kids while I read a book and drank some ice tea.

Twenty minutes later I looked up and noticed the kids running back and forth to the water with their pails, giggling. I asked "Hey, what are you two doing?" "We're scooping up the starfish with our shovels and pails and throwing them back into the ocean." Tossing another one in, they jumped up and down shouting, "You're home free!" Laughing, I went back to reading my book.

Later the clouds began to roll in and it started to get a little chilly. I grabbed my jacket and thought we should call it a day. Pops agreed. Just as my granddaughter was making her way towards the water with her pail, I looked at my watch and noticed the time. Two hours had passed. "Hey kids, we need to get going, it's getting late" I said. "But Grandma, we haven't saved all of them, yet!" they cried. "It won't make a difference, you can't possibly save them all," I said. As soon as I finished speaking, my granddaughter looked back and shouted, "Maybe not, but it makes all the difference to this one!" as she tossed the starfish into the sea.

That day I learned a valuable lesson from my grandkids that even the smallest act of kindness can make a huge difference in one's life.

This or That Activity

Below are activities you might participate in or a list of items you might bring to the beach. Go through each line and circle which one you prefer - this one - or - that one. Then when your bible study group meets, share with one another or use it as an icebreaker at the start of your meeting. Have fun!

Sunbathing	or	Swimming
Beach Towel	or	Beach Chair
Suntan Lotion	or	Suntan Oil
Two Piece	or	One Piece
Flip Flops	or	Barefoot
Beach Volleyball	or	Riding a Bike
Beach Bag	or	Beach Wagon
Cabana	or	Beach Umbrella
Beach Ball	or	Frisbee
Wide Brim Hat	or	Sun Visor
Reading a Book	or	Listening to Music
Iced Tea	or	Lemonade
Lip Balm	or	Lip Gloss
Collecting Shells	or	Building a Sandcastle
Hot Dogs	or	Burgers
Pineapple	or	Watermelon
Boogie Board	or	Surfing
Bonfire	or	BBQ
Scuba Diving	or	Snorkeling
Sunrise	or	Sunset

Day Five

As we wrap up this study, we want to revisit chapter three briefly. To refresh your memory, reread Jonah 3.

At the preaching of Jonah, the Ninevites believed God. They took His message seriously and turned away from their evil behaviors. Therefore, God withdrew from sending calamity on them. Relieved, the king and the people of Nineveh enjoyed some peace and tranquility from God's judgement. However, it should be noted, if a person (or nation) is not fully committed to God, then old behaviors tend to resurface. That's what happened to Nineveh. Over time, a new generation emerged and the people returned to their evil deeds. Their remorse was transitory. Fleeting. God's anger was once again aroused and His righteousness does not allow the guilty to go unpunished. Therefore, He later sends another prophet by the name of Nahum to speak of Nineveh's impending destruction.

Another Prophet

1. Read Nahum 1:1-8. What's going to happen to Nineveh?

2. What do you learn about God from this passage? List them below.

Seek the Lord while He may be found;
Call upon Him while He is near.
Let the wicked forsake his way,
And the unrighteous man his thoughts;
And let him return to the Lord,
And He will have compassion on him;
And to our God, for He will abundantly pardon.

Isaiah 55:6-7

Closing

God called Jonah to cry out against the wicked city of Nineveh. Instead, he fled the presence of the Lord and sailed to Tarshish. As a result, the Lord caused a raging storm on the sea and the crew worked tirelessly to save themselves and the ship, whereas Jonah was down below asleep. While the sailors tried to save their lives and Jonah's, he did little to save their souls by sharing the one true God with them. Eventually, this wayward voyage landed Jonah "entombed" in the belly of a huge fish, crying out to the Lord. God saved him and restored his life. In doing so, Jonah's ordeal will be used as a perpetual sign to point to Christ's future burial and resurrection.

God speaks to Jonah a second time to proclaim His message to the Ninevites. With renewed life, Jonah obeys. Surprisingly, the people humble themselves and turn from their evil ways. If Jonah had not shared God's word to the lost, the people would have perished. What about you? Are you willing to share God's Word to a world that desperately needs to know Him? Are you willing to warn them of impeding judgement even if they do not repent? Our Lord is a gracious and compassionate God. He is slow to anger and abundant in mercy. Will you, like Jonah...arise and go?

APPENDIX

Invite Jesus into Your Heart

Jonah...

nearly died when he was tossed into the ocean because of his sin. Had it not been for God's intervention, he would have drowned. Now entombed in the heart of the sea for three days and three nights, he cries out to God. He prays to the One who is truly able to save and restore his life. And God renews it. Three days later, Jonah finds himself on dry land.

Jesus...

in contrast, was crucified and died on a cross for all our sins. He bore the punishment for our sins and paid our debt, which we couldn't pay. He was buried in an empty tomb and laid in the heart of the earth for three days and three nights. But early Sunday morning, the stone was rolled away and Jesus rose from the dead! He is now seated at the right hand of the Father and is coming back soon.

For all have sinned and fallen short of the glory of God.
ROMANS 3:23

For God so loved the world that He gave His only begotten Son, that whosoever believes in Him should not perish, but have eternal life.
JOHN 3:16

If you confess with your mouth Jesus as Lord and believe in your heart that God raised Him from the dead, you shall be saved; for with the heart man believes, resulting in righteousness, and with the mouth he confesses, resulting in salvation.
ROMANS 10:9-10

If you've never placed your faith in Jesus Christ and invited Him into your life as your personal Lord and Savior, but would like to do so right now, please pray this prayer.

Dear God, I humbly bow my head and come before You to admit I am a sinner. I truly believe You loved me so much You sent Your Son, Jesus Christ, to die for my sins. He paid the price I could not pay. I profess Jesus as Lord and believe in my heart that You raised Him from the dead. Please forgive me of my sins. I ask Jesus to come into my heart as my personal Lord and Savior, giving me eternal life. Amen.

Tips for Hosting a Beach Themed Bible Study

1 Create a Scene

If you're lucky enough to live near the beach, then you shouldn't have any trouble decorating your surroundings. But for those who don't, don't fret. It's easy to turn your indoor (or outdoor) space into a seaside scenery. For our Jonah sign, we painted inexpensive letters and glued sea creatures onto them that we found at the dollar store.

Even our wooden sandcastle was purchased at a craft store, sprayed with adhesive glue, and sprinkled (well, actually poured) with sand over it, so it would stick. Then we sealed it with a clear acrylic spray. You can easily purchase (or borrow) coastal décor to decorate your space, so have fun with it.

2 Add Special Touches

Attention to detail can make a big difference. Whether its soft background music (instrumental or waves crashing), a lit candle in a sea shell, or a single flower in a napkin ring, it's the little things that help set the tone and leave a lasting impression. Just don't go overboard. A little goes a long way.

3 Decorate Your Table

Today, many women enjoy creating beautiful tablescapes for their family, friends, and church events (we are no different). Depending on the size of your group, you may decide to use real plates, rather than disposable plates. However, if it's more convenient, there are some very lovely paper plates on the market these days. Beautifully decorated tables are very inviting. In fact, there's something magical that happens when women walk into the room and see all the charming tables. It sets the mood and says...welcome, we've been expecting you and we are so glad you're here!

4 Get Creative with Food

What's a gathering without food? Well, not a fun one, that's for sure. If you love to cook or get creative in the kitchen, then this one's right up your alley. Go ahead, grab those cookbooks or search the internet, and get inspired by all those cute, adorable coastal bites. Even if cooking is not your thing, you can still get creative with store bought items. Our clams are wafer cookies with coral tinted icing and a candy-coated pearl, all store bought. Super simple. As the saying goes, we eat first with our eyes, and it's so true.

5 Spend Time in Prayer

Ask for any prayer requests. If you have a large group, you may decide to provide slips of paper for women to write out their requests ahead of time, so you are mindful of everyone's schedule. Encourage the women to pray for each other during the week.

Thank Everyone for Coming 6

Party favors are small parting gifts. They can be homemade or store bought, but usually depict your overall theme. Depending on your setting, you may decide to place them by each plate, on a side table, or in a basket by the door for each woman to grab on her way out, as a way of saying thank you. And if it's not in your budget, just remember, it doesn't cost you a penny to write a small thank you.

Appendix | 69

Find us at:
www.youreinvitedmag.com

www.ingramcontent.com/pod-product-compliance
Lightning Source LLC
LaVergne TN
LVHW081400060426
835510LV00016B/1910